The Little Book of
TEAMWORK

By Zack Bush and Laurie Friedman
Illustrated by Vitor Lopes

DEDICATED TO YOU –
OUR WONDERFUL READER

THIS BOOK BELONGS TO:

_____

All inquiries about this book can be sent
to the author at info@thelittlebookof.com
Published in the United States by Publishing Power, LLC
ISBN: 978-1-959141-19-8
For more information, visit our website:
www.BooksByZackAndLaurie.com
Paperback

Ready to learn more? Just turn the page.

A TEAM is a group of people who come together to achieve a common goal.

Lots of times, that goal is to win something like a game or a contest.

There are all kinds of **TEAMS.**

Some are big and have lots of players on them.

Some **TEAMS** are smaller.

Some **TEAMS** might only have two players.

Some **TEAMS** are about learning.

And some **TEAMS** are about having fun!

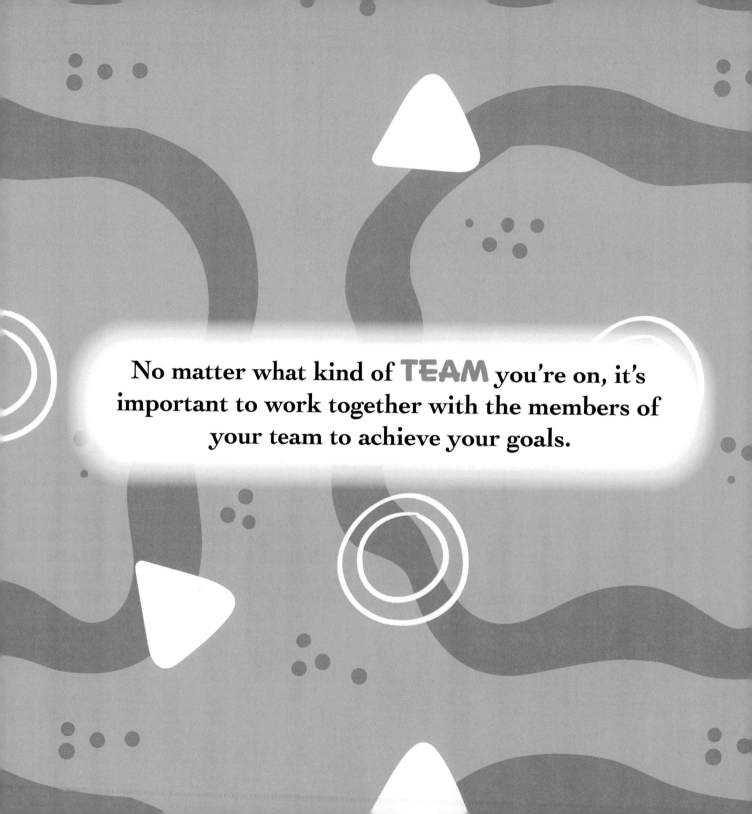

No matter what kind of **TEAM** you're on, it's important to work together with the members of your team to achieve your goals.

Think about it like this . . . when you work alone, you have to do something all by yourself.

But when you work with other people, you can accomplish
so much more!

There are so many ways you can be a great **TEAM PLAYER.** You can . . .

ENCOURAGE YOUR TEAMMATES.

Work your hardest.

Give everyone a turn.

COMPLIMENT OTHERS.

When you are part of a **TEAM**, it is important to be patient while other people on your **TEAM** learn new skills.

It is also really nice to be supportive when someone on your **TEAM** makes a mistake or does not do a good job.

Remember to always treat others how you want to be treated.

One of the best reasons to work together as a **TEAM** is that everyone on a **TEAM** has different talents and abilities.

Another thing to know about **TEAMWORK** is that it's not only about winning a game or competition. **TEAMWORK** is also important when it comes to creating and building things.

TEAMS build things like roads and bridges.

TEAMS work together to build houses where people live . . .

And buildings where people work.

TEAMS also work together to find solutions to problems.

TEAMS of scientists work together to discover ways that we can make our planet a better place for everyone to live.

TEAMS of doctors work together to find cures for diseases and help people who are sick and suffering.

TEAMS of teachers work together to find the best ways to educate students.

Even parents work together as a **TEAM** to raise their children.

And families work together to get things done at home.

Lots of good things happen when you work together with your **TEAM.** You . . .

BUILD TRUST.

LEARN NEW SKILLS.

HELP OTHERS.

HAVE FUN.

When you work well with others, you will not only feel proud of yourself. Your parents, coaches, and teachers will be proud of you too.

And when you work together with your **TEAM**, you will inspire other people to do it too!

CONGRATULATIONS!
Now you know so much about TEAMWORK.

Here's your **TEAMWORK** badge.
Go ahead. Print it out, pin it on, and start
being a team player!

Go to the website
www.BooksByZackAndLaurie.com
and print out your badges from
the Printables & Activities page.

And if you like this book, please go to
Amazon and leave a kind review.

Keep reading all of the books in #thelittlebookof series to learn new things and earn more badges.

Other books in the series include:

SOCIAL/EMOTIONAL/VALUES
The Little Book of Kindness
The Little Book of Patience
The Little Book of Confidence
The Little Book of Positivity
The Little Book of Love
The Little Book of Responsibility
The Little Book of Curiosity
The Little Book of Gratitude
The Little Book of Friendship
The Little Book of Laughter
The Little Book of Creativity
The Little Book of Honesty
The Little Book of Imagination
The Little Book of Happiness

ACTIVITIES/IDEAS
The Little Book of Camping
The Little Book of Sports
The Little Book of Music
The Little Book of Government

The Little Book of the Supreme Court
The Little Book of Transportation
The Little Book of Presidential Elections
The Little Book of Grandparents
The Little Book of Bedtime
The Little Book of Good Manners
The Little Book of Good Deeds
The Little Book of Dance
The Little Book of Yoga
The Little Book of Healthy Habits
The Little Book of Setting Goals
The Little Book of Organization

SCIENCE/NATURAL WORLD
The Little Book of Nature
The Little Book of Outer Space
The Little Book of Going Green
The Little Book of Weather
The Little Book of Pets
The Little Book of Dinosaurs

MILESTONES/HOLIDAYS
The Little Book of Kindergarten
The Little Book of First Grade
The Little Book of Valentine's Day
The Little Book of Father's Day
The Little Book of Halloween
The Little Book of Giving (Holiday Edition)
The Little Book of Santa Claus

Made in the USA
Las Vegas, NV
04 May 2024

89544299R00026